Bond

No.1 for exam success

English

10 Minute Tests

10–11+ years

OXFORD
UNIVERSITY PRESS

TEST 1: **Mixed**

Test time: 0 5 10 minutes

Rewrite these sentences changing them from plural to singular.

1 The leaves fell from the trees.

____

2 The children played with two skipping ropes and some footballs.

____

3 While playing, the kittens knocked the bags to the floor.

____

4 The swings broke and injured many children.

____

Change each of the nouns in bold to the *infinitive* of the verb.

5 Amil needed more practice with his **division**. to ____________

6 A **statement** was read out by the lawyer. to ____________

7 The **infection** had spread to Ella's ears. to ____________

8 The burglar was caught by the **detective**. to ____________

Write an *antonym* for each of these words by adding a prefix.

9 happy ____________

10 frost ____________

11 grateful ____________

12 correct ____________

13 clean ____________

14 advantage ____________

Complete the following proverbs.

15 Too many cooks ______________________________.

16 The grass is always greener ______________________________.

17 ______________________________ the mice will play.

18 ______________________________ has a silver lining.

19 The early bird ______________________________.

Write 'there', 'their' or 'they're' in the gap.

20 The children collected __________ bags before going home.

21–22 James and Sarah love __________ dog and __________ always taking him on long walks.

23 __________ is never enough money collected to help look after the homeless.

Complete these word sums. Watch out for the spelling changes!

24 busy + ly = ______________

25 argue + ment = ______________

26 laugh + ing = ______________

27 notice + able = ______________

28 complete + ly = ______________

29 imagine + ary = ______________

30 meaning + less = ______________

Total

Test 2: **Spelling**

Test time: 0 5 10 minutes

Write each of these words correctly.

1 unecessary ______________________

2 desparate ______________________

3 recomend ______________________

4 apreciate ______________________

5 haras ______________________

6 detemined ______________________

7 bargin ______________________

8 enviroment ______________________

9 interupt ______________________

10 curiocity ______________________

Add a prefix to each of these to make a new word.

11 behave ______________________

12 charge ______________________

13 cycle ______________________

14 mobile ______________________

15 ready ______________________

16 fortune ______________________

Write four words, two ending in *cial* and two ending in *tial*.

17–18 ______________________ ______________________

19–20 ______________________ ______________________

Write the plural forms of these words.

21 church ____________________

22 waltz ____________________

23 bush ____________________

24 pencil ____________________

25 wife ____________________

Add ie or ei to each of these to make a word.

26 br ___ ___ f

27 sl ___ ___ gh

28 ___ ___ ghty

29 f ___ ___ rce

30 f ___ ___ nt

31 s ___ ___ ge

32 r ___ ___ gn

33 c ___ ___ ling

Each of these words has a missing silent letter. Rewrite each word correctly.

34 nockout ____________________

35 colum ____________________

36 miniture ____________________

37 salm ____________________

38 nat ____________________

39 climer ____________________

40 nome ____________________

Total

Read this extract carefully.

Nat and the Great Bath Climb *by Penelope Lively*

Wood-lice colonies are governed by Chief Wood-lice, who are stern and ancient creatures with whiskers of immense length. Young wood-lice are kept under the most strict control by their elders; indeed they are quite literally trampled on until large enough to hold their own. Wood-lice are not creatures who go in much for expressing themselves or being original or striking out; one wood-louse acts and thinks much like another and this is the way the old wood-lice want to keep it.

From time to time the Chief Wood-louse would call the whole colony together for a meeting. The object of this meeting was for the Chief Wood-louse to lecture the newest generation of young wood-lice, who were allowed to attend as soon as their whiskers were three millimetres long, which meant they were grown-up.

The hero of this story, who was called Nat, came to his first such meeting when he was three weeks old – which in human terms is about eighteen years. The young wood-lice sat in a row at the front, feeling important but nervous, while their parents and aunts and uncles crowded behind them and the Chief Wood-louse took up a position in front.

The Chief Wood-louse looked sternly down at the **assembled** crowd and began to speak. “We are gathered together today,” he said, “to remind ourselves of the purpose of life.” He glared at the young wood-lice. “And what is the purpose of life?” The young wood-lice, who knew they were not supposed to answer, gazed at him respectfully.

“The purpose of life is to climb up the side of the bath. That is what we are here for. That is why we were born. No one has ever succeeded. But the purpose of life is to try. Each and every one of us. Your turn has now come. Your mothers and fathers have tried before you. Some brave spirits have tried several times. All have failed.”

There was silence. The young wood-lice gazed at the Chief Wood-louse and felt even more nervous and important. All except Nat, who was the youngest and smallest and had been in trouble most of his life for asking too many questions. Nat was thinking.

"You will make your attempts turn and turn about, starting with the eldest. Each of you will fail, but will have made a glorious attempt, you will then have your names inscribed on the Roll of Honour."

The young wood-lice went quite pink with pride and excitement, all except Nat, who raised one of his fourteen legs. “Please, sir,” he said, “why do we have to climb up the side of the bath?”

There was a gasp of horror from the crowd of wood-lice. Nat’s mother fainted clean away; his father bent his head in shame.

The Chief Wood-louse stared at Nat. His whiskers twitched in fury. “WHAT DID YOU SAY?”

Nat cleared his throat and repeated, politely and clearly, “Why do we have to climb up the side of the bath?”

The Chief Wood-louse huffed and puffed; his little black eyes bulged; **he creaked with indignation**. “BECAUSE IT’S THERE!” he roared...

Answer these questions about the extract.

1 Who controls young wood-lice?

2 Write a sentence describing what wood-lice elders are like.

3 How long do wood-lice whiskers have to be before wood-lice are considered to be grown-up?

4 How do you think the parents of the young wood-lice felt, waiting for the Chief Wood-louse to begin the meeting?

5 What is the meeting for?

6 Why had Nat been in trouble for most of his life?

7 What does the word **'assembled'** mean?

8 What is meant by **'he creaked with indignation'**?

9 Why were all the wood-lice shocked when Nat asked a question?

10 What do you think happened next?

Total

Test 4: **Mixed**

Test time: 0 5 10 minutes

Add to each of these words to make a compound word.

1 sun ____________

2 hand ____________

3 snow ____________

4 pen ____________

5 light ____________

6 trap ____________

7 foot ____________

8 rain ____________

Change these sentences into *indirect speech*.

9 "If we don't hurry we'll be late," shouted Zoe.

____

10 Beth enquired, "Is this the way to the toilets?"

____

11 "Quick, the guard dog is catching us!" screamed Dan.

____

____

12 "What time is it?" asked Mrs Sparks.

____

13 Mum whispered, "Remember, when you wake up in the morning it will be your birthday!"

____

____

Write a *homophone* for each of these words.

14 cereal ______________

15 great ______________

16 horse ______________

17 bough ______________

18 beach ______________

19 heard ______________

20 wait ______________

21 piece ______________

22 sent ______________

Punctuate this passage correctly. Remember to start a new line when it is needed.

23–40 Class 6 was having a swimming lesson I'm exhausted exclaimed Eva I wish something more exciting would happen I agree because if I do one more length of this pool I'll scream moaned Lee Suddenly Eva's wish came true as Mrs Davey their teacher slipped on some water at the side of the pool She fell headfirst into the pool

____

____

____

____

____

____

____

____

____

Time for a break! Go to Puzzle Page 42

Total

TEST 5: Vocabulary

Test time: 0 5 10 minutes

Write an informal equivalent for each of these words.

1 request ____________________

2 displeasure ____________________

3 unavoidable ____________________

4 discover ____________________

5 **enter** ____________________

Write six *synonyms* for the word 'said'.

6 ____________________

7 ____________________

8 ____________________

9 ____________________

10 ____________________

11 ____________________

Write a definition for each of the underlined *idioms*.

12 James felt <u>over the moon</u> when he won the trophy.

____

13 Meena was feeling <u>under the weather</u> having eaten five bags of crisps.

____

14 Ben <u>had a change of heart</u>; he didn't want to play outside in the rain!

____

Write a definition for each of these words.

15 ponder ______________________________

16 unmistakable ______________________________

17 cooperate ______________________________

18 occupation ______________________________

19 percentage ______________________________

20 submerge ______________________________

Circle the *diminutives*.

21–25 duckling calf piglet

eaglet bullock fawn

lamb owlet foal

Complete each sentence as a *simile*.

26 Aimee's bed was as warm as ______________________________.

27 Jacob ran as fast as ______________________________.

28 The custard was as thick as ______________________________.

29 Jess felt as cold as ______________________________.

30 Tom's bruise was as big as ______________________________.

Total

Test 6: **Mixed**

Test time: 0 5 10 minutes

Circle the silent letter in each of these words.

1 guilt

2 knuckle

3 rhombus

4 island

5 gnat

6 crescent

7 crumb

8 answer

What are the following: commands, questions or statements?

9 Put your homework on the table ________________

10 What time is our appointment ________________

11 Global warming is a serious problem ________________

12 It's six o'clock ________________

13 Where have I put my recorder ________________

14 Sit quietly ________________

Add the missing apostrophes.

15–16 Ill run and get my coat from Henrys house.

17 Wheres my hat?

18 Isnt it time the cinema doors opened?

Write four words used in English but derived from another language. Example: croissant

19 ____________________

20 ____________________

21 ____________________

22 ____________________

What parts of speech are each of these words?

23 after ____________________

24 scream ____________________

25 he ____________________

26 tarantula ____________________

27 frantically ____________________

Write three sentences, each using the given phrases.

28 as a consequence

____

29 on the other hand

____

30 in contrast to

____

Total

TEST 7: **Grammar**

Test time: 0 5 10 minutes

Write two examples of each of the following.

1–2 common nouns ______________ ______________

3–4 abstract nouns ______________ ______________

5–6 proper nouns ______________ ______________

7–8 collective nouns ______________ ______________

Fill each gap with an *adverb*.

9 Matthew looked ______________ at the sweets.

10 Hannah copied her story ______________.

11 The Gallop family ______________ waved goodbye to their cousins.

12 Jacob ______________ tidied his messy room.

Write two *adjectives* to describe each of these nouns.

13–14 ______________, ______________ hair

15–16 a ______________, ______________ lion

17–18 a ______________, ______________ butterfly

Write two sentences that begin with *fronted adverbials*.

19 ____

20 ____

Underline the *preposition* in each sentence.

21 Shall we meet after breakfast?

22 Jessica's cat slept on her bed.

23 Let's see how far we can swim under the water.

24 Carl jumped over the broken gate.

Write three sentences, each with a *comparative adjective* and a *conjunction*.

25–26 ______________________________

____

____

27–28 ______________________________

____

____

29–30 ______________________________

____

____

Total

Test time: 0 5 10 minutes

Read this poem carefully.

The Sands of Dee

"O Mary, go and call the cattle home,
And call the cattle home,
And call the cattle home,
Across the sands of Dee;"
The western wind was wild and dank with foam,
And all alone went she.

The western tide crept up along the sand,
And o'er and o'er the sand,
And round and round the sand,
As far as eye could see.
The rolling mist came down and hid the land:
And never home came she.

"Oh, is it weed, or fish, or floating hair –
A tress of golden hair,
A drowned maiden's hair
Above the nets at sea?
Was never salmon yet that shone so fair
Among the stakes on Dee."

They rowed her in across the rolling foam,
The cruel, crawling foam,
The cruel, hungry foam,
To her grave beside the sea:
But still the boatmen hear her call the cattle home,
Across the sands of Dee.

by Charles Kingsley

Answer these questions about the poem.

1 What was Mary asked to do?

2 When Mary set off, what was the weather like?

3 'The rolling mist came down and hid the land:'
What image does this line conjure up in your mind?

4 Copy the line in the poem that informs us of Mary's death.

5 Why do you think the sea foam is described as cruel?

6 Where was Mary buried?

7 Which word in the poem means damp or moist?

8 What does 'o'er' mean?

9 How do you think Mary felt when she was sent out to the sands of Dee?

10 Describe how this poem makes you feel.

Time for a break! Go to Puzzle Page 43

Total

Test 9: **Mixed**

Test time: 0 5 10 minutes

Underline the correct verb form in each sentence.

1 When (is/are) we going to get to Gran's house?

2 (Is/Are) we meeting this afternoon?

3 Todd's parents (was/were) pleased with his progress.

4 It (was/were) raining outside.

5 Which pony (is/are) Jodie's?

Add *tious* or *cious* to complete each word.

6 suspi ____________________

7 infec ____________________

8 ambi ____________________

9 vi ____________________

10 nutri ____________________

Write each of these words correctly.

11 embarras ____________________

12 seperate ____________________

13 marvelous ____________________

14 vegtable ____________________

15 resturant ____________________

Write a short conversation between two friends discussing what they might do after school. Be careful to start new lines when they are needed and to punctuate the conversation correctly.

16–25

____

____

____

____

____

____

____

____

____

____

Write five *synonyms* for the word 'nice'.

26 __________

27 __________

28 __________

29 __________

30 __________

Total

Test 10: **Sentences**

Test time: 0 5 10 minutes

Write these statements as questions.

1 The water is too deep to swim in.

____

2 Andy is hiding in the woods.

____

3 Bola isn't allowed out on his bike.

____

4 My birthday is in February.

____

5 It takes Sophie thirty minutes to walk to school.

____

Write two sentences. Each sentence needs to have two commas.

6–7 ____

____

8–9 ____

____

Rewrite this short passage correctly. Remember to begin a new line when a different person starts to speak.

10–20 Is it Gym Club tonight asked Thomas It always is on Monday replied Poppy Thomas groaned he'd forgotten his PE kit again

____

____

____

Rewrite these sentences without double negatives.

21 We didn't want no homework.

____

22 Jake hasn't no problem learning his spellings.

____

23 Dad couldn't find no gap in which to park his car.

____

Write two sentences that indicate parenthesis using commas, brackets or dashes.

24 ____

25 ____

Total

TEST 11: **Mixed**

Test time: 0 5 10 minutes

Draw lines to link each old word with the modern word.

1	saith	are
2	remaineth	here
3	hither	says
4	abides	remain
5	art	lives

Complete each sentence with a *phrase* or *clause*.

6 Miss James ______________________________

______________________________ waited for the class to listen.

7 The cat ______________________________

______________________________ pounced on its prey.

8 Todd's computer ______________________________

______________________________ frequently broke down.

9 The policeman ______________________________

______________________________ kept an eye on the man.

10 The sun ______________________________

______________________________ melted the ice cream in minutes.

Write two words, at least one hyphenated, using each of these prefixes.

11–12 bi ______________ ______________

13–14 non ______________ ______________

15–16 cross ______________ ______________

17–18 co ______________ ______________

19–20 re ______________ ______________

Fill each gap with an *adjective* and noun.

21 Sam screamed and ran from the ______________________________.

22 Jack snuggled closer to the ______________________________.

23 Freda rushed towards the ______________________________.

24 Joseph raced after the ______________________________.

Add 'able' or 'ible' to complete each word.

25 charge________

26 irresist________

27 convert________

28 extend________

29 regrett________

30 avoid________

Total

TEST 12: **Spelling**

Test time: 0 5 10 minutes

List five *ough* words. Each word must illustrate a different pronunciation of the *ough* letter pattern.

1–5 ____________________

____

____

____

____

Write each of these words correctly.

6 imediately ____________________

7 relevent ____________________

8 secratary ____________________

9 temprature ____________________

10 excellant ____________________

Add ance or ence to each of these to make a word.

11 appear________

12 eleg________

13 radi________

14 occurr________

15 sil________

16 experi________

Add ant or ent to each of these to make a word.

17 pleas________

18 hesit________

19 magnific________

20 abund________

21 stagn________

22 transpar________

TEST 1: Mixed (pages 2–3)

1 **The <u>leaf</u> fell from the <u>tree</u>.** If a word ends in '-f' or '-fe', add 'ves' to form the plural. (There are some exceptions, such as 'cliffs'.) If a word ends in a vowel, add 's'.

2 **The <u>child</u> played with <u>a</u> skipping <u>rope</u> and <u>a football</u>.** Some words change completely as plurals, e.g. child – children, mouse – mice.

3 **While playing, the <u>kitten</u> knocked the <u>bag</u> to the floor.**

4 **The <u>swing</u> broke and injured <u>a child</u>.** Refer to Q2.

5–8 Refer to definition of infinitives in key words on page 47.

5 **to divide** 6 **to state**
7 **to infect** 8 **to detect**

9–14 Refer to definition of antonyms in key words on page 47. A prefix is a group of letters added to the beginning of a root word to make a new word.

9 **unhappy** 10 **defrost**
11 **ungrateful** 12 **incorrect**
13 **unclean** 14 **disadvantage**

15–19 A proverb is a well-known saying.

15 **Too many cooks spoil the broth.**
16 **The grass is always greener on the other side.**
17 **While the cat's away the mice will play.**
18 **Every cloud has a silver lining.**
19 **The early bird catches the worm.**

20–23 A quick way of remembering which word to use is that 'there' is connected to the words 'here' and 'where'. An apostrophe shows where there are missing letters in a contraction so 'they're' is a shortened form of 'they are'. 'Their' means 'belonging to them'.

20 **their** The children collected their bags before going home.

21–22 **their**, **they're** James and Sarah love their dog and they're always taking him on long walks.

23 **There** There is never enough money collected to help look after the homeless.

24 **busily** When adding the suffix '-ly', just add it to the root word unless it ends in a 'y', which should then change to an 'i'; if the root word ends in '-le', change the '-le' to '-ly'.

25 **argument** The suffix '-ment' can usually be added to the root word with no spelling change; however, as in this example, there are some exceptions (in this case, the 'e' has been removed).

26 **laughing** When adding the suffix '-ing', just add it to the root word. There are some exceptions: if the root word ends in '-e', it is sometimes removed (e.g. 'love' becomes 'loving'); if the root word ends in a short vowel and consonant, double the consonant before adding '-ing' (e.g. 'run' becomes 'running')

27 **noticeable** When adding the suffix '-able', just add it to the root word. There are some exceptions; if the root word ends in '-e', it is sometimes removed, e.g. 'love' becomes 'lovable'. However, this word is an exception to this exception!

28 **completely** Refer to Q24.

29 **imaginary** As with many suffixes, '-ary' can usually be added to the root word without any changes, unless the root word ends in an '-e', which is then removed.

30 **meaningless** The suffix '-less' can generally be added to the root word without any change in spelling.

TEST 2: Spelling (pages 4–5)

1 **unnecessary** 2 **desperate**
3 **recommend** 4 **appreciate**
5 **harass** 6 **determined**
7 **bargain** 8 **environment**
9 **interrupt** 10 **curiosity**

11–16 Refer to Test 1 Mixed Q9–14.

11 *misbehave* 12 *recharge*
13 *tricycle* 14 *automobile*
15 *unready* 16 *misfortune*

17–20 In most cases, 'tial' is used if it follows a consonant, and 'cial' is used if it follows a vowel. (There are some exceptions, such as 'spatial'.)

17–18 Possible answers: *special*, *official*

19–20 Possible answers: *partial*, *substantial*

21 **churches** If a word ends in '-s', '-sh', '-ch', '-x' or '-z', add 'es' to form the plural.

22 **waltzes** Refer to Q21.

23 **bushes** Refer to Q21.

24 **pencils** For words not ending in '-s', '-sh', '-ch', '-x' or '-z', add 's'.

25 **wives** Refer to Test 1 Mixed Q1.

26–33 Although the general 'i before e except after c' rule can be applied sometimes, there are many exceptions. When the sound is ee, use 'ie' (e.g. belief); when the sound is ay, use 'ei' (e.g. neighbour). As usual, there are also some exceptions to this rule, such as caffeine.

26 br**ie**f The ee sound means it is spelt 'ie'.

27 sl**e**igh The ay sound means it is spelt 'ei'.

28 **e**ighty Refer to Q27.
29 fi**e**rce Refer to Q26.
30 f**e**int Refer to Q27.
31 si**e**ge Refer to Q26.
32 r**e**ign Refer to Q27.
33 c**e**iling 'i before e, except after c.'
34 **k**nockout
35 colum**n**
36 mini**a**ture
37 **p**salm
38 **g**nat
39 clim**b**er
40 **g**nome

TEST 3: Comprehension (pages 6–7)

1 **their elders** (line 5)
2 *Wood-lice elders are strict and set in their ways*. (lines 5 and 10–12)
3 **3 millimetres** (para 2 line 7)
4 *proud that their young were attending the meeting but also probably a little nervous*
5 *to remind themselves of the purpose of life* (para 4 lines 4–5)
6 *asking too many questions* (para 6 lines 5–6)
7 *brought together*
8 *he moved with displeasure*
9 *because nobody ever asked the Chief Wood-louse questions*
10 Child's own answer. This could include other Wood-louse asking questions, or watching each Wood-lice climb the bath, or Nat's parents withdrawing him from the meeting in embarrassment.

TEST 4: Mixed (pages 8–9)

1–8 A compound word is a word formed from two other words. Possible answers include the following:
1 *sunlight* 2 *handbag*
3 *snowball* 4 *penknife*
5 *lighthouse* 6 *trapdoor*
7 *football* 8 *rainfall*
9–13 Refer to definition of indirect speech in key words on page 47.
9 **Zoe shouted that if we didn't hurry we'd be late.** The contractions may be written as two words, e.g. 'did not' instead of 'didn't'.
10 **Beth enquired whether that was the way to the toilets.**
11 **Dan screamed that we had to be quick as the guard dog was catching us.** A different conjunction with a similar meaning may be used instead of 'as', such as 'because'.
12 **Mrs Sparks asked what time it was.**
13 **Mum whispered to remind me that when I woke up in the morning it would be my birthday.** The word order may be slightly different, e.g. 'Mum whispered that I should remember when I woke up…'
14–22 Refer to definition of homophones in key words on page 47.
14 **serial** 15 **grate**
16 **hoarse** 17 **bow**
18 **beech** 19 **herd**
20 **weight** 21 **peace**
22 **scent** or **cent**
23–40 Class 6 was having a swimming lesson.
"I'm exhausted," exclaimed Eva. "I wish something more exciting would happen."
"I agree because if I do one more length of this pool I'll scream!" moaned Lee.
Suddenly, Eva's wish came true as Mrs Davey, their teacher, slipped on some water at the side of the pool. She fell headfirst into the pool!

TEST 5: Vocabulary (pages 10–11)

1 *ask for*
2 *unhappiness*
3 *unable to avoid*
4 *find out*
5 *go in*
6–11 Refer to definition of synonyms in key words on page 47. Possible answers include *cried*, *exclaimed*, *laughed*, *replied*, *shouted*
12–14 Refer to definition of idioms in key words on page 47.
12 *very pleased*
13 *sick or ill*
14 *changed his mind*
15–20 Any definition that approximates the ones given below is acceptable.
15 *to think carefully about something*
16 *clear, obvious*
17 *to work willingly with others*
18 *a job or something to fill one's time*
19 *something divided into a hundred parts*
20 *to go under water*
21–25 **duckling**, **piglet**, **eaglet**, **bullock**, **owlet**. Refer to definition of diminutives in key words on page 47.
26–30 Refer to definition of similes in key words on page 47. Possible answers include:
26 *toast*
27 *a cheetah*
28 *cement*
29 *ice*
30 *an apple*

TEST 6: Mixed (pages 12–13)

1 **u**	2 **k**	3 **h**
4 **s**	5 **g**	6 **c**
7 **b**	8 **w**	

9–14 Commands begin with an imperative verb and tend to omit the subject of the sentence, e.g. “Eat your dinner.” Questions usually begin with a question word and require a response. Statements generally contain a subject, verb and object.

9 **command**	10 **question**
11 **statement**	12 **statement**
13 **question**	14 **command**

15–18 Apostrophes are used for contractions (also known as for omission, when two words are combined and a letter is omitted)' e.g. 'do not' becomes 'don't', with the apostrophe indicating the missing o, and to show possession, e.g. the shoe belonging to Joe = Joe's shoe.

15–16 **<u>I'll</u> run and get my coat from <u>Henry's</u> house.** Contraction of 'I' + 'will' and possession.

17 **<u>Where's</u> my hat?** Contraction of 'Where' + 'is'.

18 **<u>Isn't</u> it time the cinema doors opened?** Contraction of 'Is' + 'not'.

19–22 Possible answers include *pizza*, *origami*, *umbrella*, *siesta*.

23 **preposition or conjunction** e.g. 'I ate tea after 5pm' or 'I ate tea after I cleaned my room'

24 **verb or noun** e.g. 'I scream' or 'I heard a scream'

25 **pronoun**

26 **noun**

27 **adverb**

28–30 Child's own answers.

TEST 7: Grammar (pages 14–15)

1–2 A common noun is a noun referring to a person, place or thing – it is not capitalised. Possible answers include *chair*, *house*.

3–4 Refer to definition of abstract nouns in key words on page 47. Possible answers include *love*, *beauty*.

5–6 A proper noun is a noun referring to the name of something – it is capitalised. Possible answers include *Beth*, *England*.

7–8 Refer to definition of collective nouns in key words on page 47. Possible answers include *crowd*, *gaggle*.

9–12 Refer to definition of adverbs in key words on page 47. Here are some possible answers:

9 *longingly*	10 *neatly*
11 *sadly*	12 *grumpily*

13–18 Refer to definition of adjectives in key words on page 47. Here are some possible answers:

13–14 *long, black*

15–16 *large, snarling*

17–18 *small, fragile*

19–20 Refer to definition of fronted adverbials in key words on page 47. A possible answer could be *Under the stairs, he found a large hole*.

21–24 Refer to definition of prepositions in key words on page 47.

21 **after**	22 **on**
23 **under**	24 **over**

25–30 Refer to definitions of comparative adjectives and conjunctions in key words on page 47. Child's own answers must include one of each per sentence. An example sentence would be *The girl was tall, <u>even though</u> she was <u>younger</u> than the others*.

TEST 8: Comprehension (pages 16–17)

1 **call the cattle home** (lines 1–3)

2 *there was a wild wind* (line 5)

3 Child's own answers. This could include interpretations of personification, such as the weather purposely hiding the land to make it difficult for Mary to return.

4 **A drowned maiden's hair** (line 15)

5 *it was the sea foam in which Mary died*

6 *beside the sea* (line 22)

7 **dank** (line 5)

8 **over**

9 Child's own answer, e.g. *nervous*.

10 Child's own answer.

TEST 9: Mixed (pages 18–19)

1 When **are** we going to get to Gran's house?

2 **Are** we meeting this afternoon?

3 Todd's parents **were** pleased with his progress.

4 It **was** raining outside.

5 Which pony **is** Jodie's?

6–10 The suffix '-tious' is usually used when the root word can also have a '-tion' ending. If the root word ends in '-ce', the suffix '-cious' is usually used (of course, there are exceptions).

6 **suspicious**

7 **infectious** The word 'infec<u>tion</u>' can also be made from the root word.

8 **ambitious** The word 'ambi<u>tion</u>' can also be made from the root word.

9 **vicious** The root word is 'vi<u>ce</u>'.

10 **nutritious** The word 'nutri<u>tion</u>' can also be made from the root word.

11 **embarrass**
12 **separate**
13 **marvellous**
14 **vegetable**
15 **restaurant**
16–25 Child's own answer. Give marks for correct layout and punctuation.
26–30 Refer to definition of synonyms in key words on page 47. Possible answers include: *pleasant*, *lovely*, *enjoyable*, *good*, *likeable*.

TEST 10: Sentences (pages 20–21)

1 **Is the water too deep to swim in?**
2 **Is Andy hiding in the woods?**
3 **Isn't Bola allowed out on his bike?**
4 **Is my birthday in February?**
5 **Does it take Sophie thirty minutes to walk to school?**
6–9 Commas are used to separate items in a list. There is a comma between each item except for the final two, which are separated by 'and' instead. Commas are also used to separate the main clause in a sentence from the additional added information. Child's own answers.
10–20 "Is it Gym Club tonight?" asked Thomas. "It always is on Monday," replied Poppy. Thomas groaned. He'd forgotten his PE kit again.
21 **We didn't want any homework**.
22 **Jake hasn't a problem learning his spellings**. or **Jake has no problem learning his spellings**.
23 **Dad couldn't find a gap in which to park his car**. or **Dad could find no gap in which to park his car**.
24–25 Refer to definition of parenthesis in key words on page 47. For example: *Jess and her friends (Aman and Janice) caught the bus to town*.

TEST 11: Mixed (pages 22–23)

1 **saith – says**
2 **remaineth – remain**
3 **hither – here**
4 **abides – lives**
5 **art – are**
6–10 Refer to definitions of phrases and clauses in key words on page 47. Child's own answers.
11–20 Refer to Test 1 Mixed Q9–14. Here are some possible answers.
11–12 *bi-monthly, bicycle*
13–14 *non-smoker, nonsense*
15–16 *cross-section, crossroad*
17–18 *co-operate, coexist*
19–20 *re-cover, rewrite*
21–24 Refer to definition of adjectives in key words on page 47. Possible answers include:
21 *haunted house*
22 *crackling fire*
23 *shoe shop*
24 *small dog*
25–30 As a general rule (although there are exceptions), if the root word looks like a whole word, the suffix will most likely be '-able'; if the root word does not look like a whole word, the suffix will most likely be '-ible'.
25 **chargeable**
26 **irresistible**
27 **convertible** An exception to the rule.
28 **extendable**
29 **regrettable**
30 **avoidable**

TEST 12: Spelling (pages 24–25)

1–5 Pronunciations of *ough* include *through, rough, cough, thought, bough*. Other possible answers include *bought, borough, enough*.
6 **immediately**
7 **relevant**
8 **secretary**
9 **temperature**
10 **excellent**
11–22 The suffixes '-ant'/'-ance' and '-ent'/'-ence' are particularly difficult to work out as they are pronounced the same and there is no hard and fast rule to distinguish between them. If a root word can use '-ation' as a suffix, then '-ant'/'-ance' are most likely used.
11 **appearance**
12 **elegance**
13 **radiance** As per rule (radi<u>ation</u>).
14 **occurrence**
15 **silence**
16 **experience**
17 **pleasant**
18 **hesitant** As per rule (hesit<u>ation</u>).
19 **magnificent**
20 **abundant**
21 **stagnant** As per rule (stagn<u>ation</u>).
22 **transparent**
23–29 Refer to definition of root word in key words on page 47.
23 **garden**
24 **ornament**
25 **resist**
27 **shine**
28 **happy**
29 **alter**
30 **giraffe**
31 **pulley**

32 **grammar**
33 **professor**
34 **necessary**
35 **wrapping**
36–40 In '-fer' root word endings, when the second syllable is stressed (once the suffix has been added), the last 'r' is doubled. When the first syllable is stressed, the root word spelling remains the same.
36 **preferring**
37 **referral**
38 **preference**
39 **transferred**
40 **referring**

TEST 13: Comprehension (pages 26–27)

1 **pedigree** (lines 1–2)
2 *they are traditionally bred to work* (lines 9–11)
3 **plenty of exercise** (lines 19–20)
4 **when both parents are known** (section 2 lines 7–8)
5 *Cross-bred dogs are cheaper to buy, stronger in constitution and less highly strung* (section 2 lines 4, 12 and 13)
6 *mixed ancestry – a mix of different dog breeds* (section 3 line 1)
7 *it's hard to predict accurately how they will develop since their sires are unknown* (section 2 lines 5–7)
8 Child's own answer, for example, mongrel dogs because most of them make affectionate companions (section 3 line 3)
9 *offspring*
10 *sturdy*

TEST 14: Mixed (pages 28–29)

1 **bushes** Refer to Test 2 Spelling Q21.
2 **athletes** Refer to Test 2 Spelling Q24.
3 **convoys** Refer to Q2.
4 **motifs** Refer to Test 1 Mixed Q1 (this is an exception).
5 **kangaroos** Refer to Q2.
6 **babies** For words ending in 'y', change the 'y' to 'i' and add 'es'.
7–9 Refer to definition of mnemonic in key words on page 47. Child's own answers, e.g. unnecessary = *using new napkins eight children eat sugary sweets and raspberry yoghurts*.
10–14 Refer to Test 10 Sentences Q6–9.
10–11 Grandad, who was feeling grumpy anyway, got really cross when the puppy chewed his new slippers.
12–13 Take a few moments to listen to different sounds – perhaps the sound of the wind howling, sirens screaming, leaves rustling or buzzing planes.
14 To be able to understand your own beliefs and values, you need to learn about the beliefs and values of others.
15–24 A suffix is a group of letters added to the end of a root word to make a new word. Here are some possible answers.
15–16 *friendly, friendship*
17–18 *shameful, shameless*
19–20 *happiness, happily*
21–22 *painful, painless*
23–24 *greatness, greatly*
25 A colon is often used before a list or quotation – the first clause must be independent. For example: *We have two types of tree in our garden: beech and oak.*
26 A semicolon can be used to join two clauses, often related, together. For example: *It's snowing; I'm so excited*.
27–30 A semicolon can also be used to list expanded noun phrases. For example: *People enjoy summer for a number of reasons: it's warm; they enjoy doing things outside; they can eat BBQs; it stays light late into the evening*.

TEST 15: Vocabulary (pages 30–31)

1–5 Child's own sentences. Five sentences containing the listed words.
6 **husband**
7 **prince**
8 **nephew**
9 **gentleman** or **lord**
10 **lion**
11 **fox**
12–15 **television, DVD player, astronaut, website.** Children can work this out by choosing the nouns that identify modern inventions, occupations or ideas.
16–20 Refer to definition of abbreviation in key words on page 47.
16 **compact disc**
17 **kilogram**
18 **United States of America**
19 **South East or Stock Exchange**
20 **Member of Parliament or Military Police**
21–22 Possible answers include *outfit*, *outlaw*
23–24 Possible answers include *thrill*, *throne*
25–26 Possible answers include *disgrace*, *dispatch*
27–30 Refer to definition of metaphor in key words on page 47. Here are some possible answers:
27 *The wind was a howling beast.*
28 *The snow is soft balls of cotton wool.*
29 *The leaves are a prickly carpet.*
30 *His bedroom was a tip!*

TEST 16: Mixed (pages 32–33)

1–8 Refer to Test 7 Grammar Q1–8. Possible answers include *man* (common noun), *Lucy* (proper noun), *appearance* (abstract noun), *bunch* (collective noun).

9–12 Direct speech is written in inverted commas (speech marks) and is often followed or preceded by a reporting clause so the reader knows who has spoken (e.g. 'said Mum', or 'I whispered').

9 **"Ben, it is time to put the chips in the oven," called Mum.** 'It is' may be written as 'it's'.

10 **"There's nothing to worry about," said the vet.** 'Said the vet' may be replaced with 'the vet told me'.

11 **"It's time for lunch," announced Mrs Owen.** 'It's' may be written as 'it is'.

12 **"Rupesh, would you like to stay the night at my house?" asked Ryan.** This could also be written as *"Would you like to stay the night at my house?" Ryan asked Rupesh.*

13 As this is not hyphenated (like man-eating shark), 'man' must be used as a noun, e.g. *Man eating shark shocks local villagers*.

14 As this is hyphenated, the phrase must be used to show a bottle holding hot-water, rather than a hot (temperature) water bottle, e.g. *Sarah felt ill so she made herself a hot-water bottle*.

15 As this is not hyphenated, this word must be used to mean finding something or returning to health, as opposed to covering something again (re-cover), e.g. *If I get some rest, I may recover*.

16 As this is hyphenated, the phrase must be used to identify the manager of a small business, rather than a business manager who is small, e.g. *Anshul was a successful small-business manager*.

17 As this is not hyphenated, the phrase must be used to show a metal detector that is heavy, rather than something that detects heavy metals, e.g. *I felt so weak that I couldn't carry my heavy metal detector*.

18–22 Refer to definition of simile in key words on page 47. Here are some possible answers.

18 *The water was as blue as sapphire.*

19 *The swan was as white as snow.*

20 The drum was as loud as a thunder clap.

21 *Jo saw a spider that was as big as a house.*

22 *The monkey sat as quiet as a mouse.*

23–30 Refer to definition of root word in key words on page 47.

23 **marine** The prefix 'sub' has been added.

24 **claim** The prefix 'ex' has been added.

25 **post** The suffix 'age' has been added.

26 **digest** The suffix 'ible' has been added.

27 **rely** The suffix 'able' has been added.

28 **nation** The prefix 'inter' and suffix 'al' has been added.

29 **hygiene** The suffix 'ic' has been added.

30 **offence** The suffix 'ive' has been added.

TEST 17: Grammar (pages 34–35)

1–10 Refer to definition of adverb in key words on page 47. Here are some possible answers.

1–2 *ran quickly*

3–4 *worked slowly*

5–6 *searched helplessly*

7–8 *sat patiently*

9–10 *talked quietly*

11–15 Refer to definition of conjunction in key words on page 47. Child's own answers, e.g. Molly loved her party dress <u>*because*</u> *it had pockets* or <u>*but*</u> *hated her shoes*, etc.

16–20 Refer to definition of adjectival phrase in key words on page 47. Here are some possible answers.

16 *an unusually large banana*

17 *the extremely naughty children*

18 *a scary black spider*

19 *the surprisingly calm wind*

20 *a really exciting computer game*

21–30 Refer to definitions of abstract noun, preposition, pronoun and superlative on page 47. Possible answers include:

21–22 *friendship, hatred*

23–24 *above, under*

25–26 *(to) sit, (to) laugh*

27–28 *it, he*

29–30 *smallest, largest*

TEST 18: Comprehension (pages 36–37)

1 **The Second World War** (para 2 lines 1–3)

2 *He let him win at marbles; he lent him his wicket keeper's gloves; he gave him his best stamp* (para 4 lines 6–8)

3 *when he arrived at school with grazed knees, dirt on his blazer and red eyes from crying* (para 4 lines 13–15)

4 *because the boy's father was an electrician rather than being at the front line* (para 5 lines 11–13)

5 Child's own answer, for example, *because he didn't stand up for his dead father or defend his honour*

6 **He worked in a button factory** (para 7 lines 2–3)

7 Child's own answer, for example, *He might have felt like he was being strong and tough.*
8 *He was hiding his embarrassment about the fact that his father hadn't gone off to fight in the war.*
9 Child's own answer
10 *Most men were going off to fight in the war, and those who died were thought of as heroes.*

TEST 19: Mixed (pages 38–39)

1–4 Refer to Test 1 Mixed Q15–19.
1 *Two people can be more successful at doing something than one person.*
2 *You get better at something with practice.*
3 *If you help me, I will help you.*
4 *It is best not to change things.*
5–11 **"Can I open my present now?" asked Gina. "I have waited a very long time!"**
12–16 **"Let's go ice-skating," suggested Jenny.** An exclamation mark may be used instead of a comma.
17–22 Refer to definition of onomatopoeic in key words on page 47. Possible answers include:
17–18 *crash, whoosh*
19–20 *hissing, slithering*
21–22 *whizz, fizzle*
23 **pronoun**
24 **conjunction**
25 **adverb**
26 **verb or noun** *I hate eggs* or *The cat hissed with hate.*
27 **verb**
28–30 Refer to Test 6 Mixed Q9–14. Child's own answers.

TEST 20: Sentences (pages 40–41)

1–5 The verb *was* follows the subject when it is a singular noun; when it is plural, the verb *were* should be used instead.
1 **was or were** 'Family' is a collective noun and can be considered either singular or plural.
2 **was** 'The ball' is singular.
3 **were** 'Children' is plural.
4 **was** 'The villain' is singular.
5 **was** 'Hannah' is singular.
6–8 Refer to definitions of phrase and clause in key words on page 47. Child's own answers, for example, *The horses, <u>tired and hungry</u>, waited for their morning feed*. 'Tired and hungry' is a phrase as it does not contain a main verb.
9–10 Refer to definition of relative clause in key words on page 47. Child's own answers, for example, *The girl, who had long blonde hair, sat on a chair*.
11–15 "Quieten down!" bellowed the headteacher.
16–18 Darren raced towards the ball, not wanting to be beaten by anyone.
19–23 "Are we going to win?" called Helen.
24–26 In an active sentence, the subject is doing something ('The boy rode the horse.'). In a passive sentence, the subject is having something done to it ('The horse was ridden by the boy.'). A passive sentence often uses the word 'was' before the verb. Child's own answers, for example, *The dog was being walked by the boy*.
27 **<u>D</u>**ave's cats, **<u>B</u>**atman and **<u>R</u>**obin, tore up his **<u>H</u>**arry **<u>P</u>**otter poster.
28 **<u>T</u>**he train was late, eventually arriving in **<u>M</u>**anchester after **<u>M</u>**anchester **<u>U</u>**nited had won their match!

Puzzle 1 (page 42)

1 **South Africa**
2 **department store**
3 **Downing Street**
4 **pencil crayon**
5 **shopping trolley**
6 **Prince William**
7 **swimming costume**
8 **Blue Peter**
A and B Child's own answers

Puzzle 2 (page 43)

A 'soft c' is the letter 'c' pronounced as a s sound; a 'soft g' is the letter 'g' pronounces as a j sound. Soft cs and gs often precede the letters 'i', 'y' or 'e'.
necessary, innocent, receive, decision
gaol, religion, vegetable, imagination

Puzzle 3 (page 44)

Word families are those formed from the same root word (see p47 for a definition of root word). Here are some possible answers.
happy – happily, happiest, unhappy
phone – telephone, microphone, phoneme
question – questioning, questionable, questioned
detect – detective, detecting, detectable
graph – telegraph, autograph, photograph

Puzzle 4 (page 45)

Child's own answers

Puzzle 5 (page 46)

Across
- 2 **bicycle**
- 3 **triathlon**
- 5 **octopus**
- 6 **decade**

Down
- 1 **octagon**
- 4 **tripod**

Write the *root word* of each of these words.

23 gardener ______________________

24 ornamental ______________________

25 resistance ______________________

26 noticeable ______________________

27 shiny ______________________

28 happiness ______________________

29 alteration ______________________

Add the missing double letters to each of these words.

30 gira__ __e

31 pu__ __ey

32 gra__ __ar

33 profe__ __or

34 nece__ __ary

35 wra__ __ing

Complete these word sums. Watch out for the spelling changes!

36 prefer + ing = ______________________

37 refer + al = ______________________

38 prefer + ence = ______________________

39 transfer + ed = ______________________

40 refer + ing = ______________________

Time for a break! Go to Puzzle Page 44

Total

Test time: 0 5 10 minutes

Read this extract carefully.

Pedigree or mongrel?

Pedigree dogs

Pedigree, or pure-bred, dogs are the most expensive to buy, but it is not usually difficult to find homes for their puppies. Being highly bred may make them more delicate than dogs of mixed ancestry and more likely to inherit defects. The very fact that they are descended from a line of dogs used traditionally for a particular form of work may make some of them unsuitable as pets for the average household. Dalmatians, for instance, were once carriage dogs. A pair of them would run alongside the horses in the capacity of outriders. Their elegant proportions and attractive, spotted coats mean they are now in demand as pets, but they should only be kept if they can be allowed plenty of exercise.

Cross-bred dogs

Cross-breds are the **progeny** of two pure-bred parents of different breeds. Cross-breds usually make very good pets. They are cheaper to buy, but of course cost as much to keep as pedigree dogs. When both parents are known, it is possible to estimate the adult size and type of cross-bred puppy. Depending on the combination of the parents' characteristics, a cross-bred dog can be very attractive, and may be stronger in constitution and often less highly strung than either of its parents.

Mongrel dogs

Mongrels are dogs of mixed ancestry. They are inexpensive and most make affectionate companions. Nearly all mongrels are **robust**, but since their sires are often unknown, it is impossible to predict accurately how mongrel puppies will develop. This is one reason why mongrels are difficult to home, and why so many are taken to animal welfare societies, such as the RSPCA, from which they can sometimes be adopted.

The Official RSPCA Pet Guide

Care for Your Dog

Answer these questions about the extract.

1 Which type of dog is most expensive to buy?

____

2 Why are some pedigree dogs unsuitable to keep as pets for the average household?

____

3 If a Dalmatian is kept as a pet what does it particularly need?

____

4 When is it possible to estimate the adult size of a cross-bred dog?

____

5 Write three differences between pedigree and cross-bred dogs.

____

____

6 Describe the parents of a mongrel dog.

____

7 Why are some mongrel dogs difficult to home?

____

8 Which type of dog would you choose to keep and why?

____

____

9 What is meant by the word **'progeny'**?

____

10 What does **'robust'** mean? ______________________________

Total

TEST 14: **Mixed**

Test time: 0 5 10 minutes

Write each of these nouns in its plural form.

1 bush ____________

2 athlete ____________

3 convoy ____________

4 motif ____________

5 kangaroo ____________

6 baby ____________

Write a *mnemonic* to help you remember how to spell each of these words.

7 accommodate

____

8 government

____

9 unnecessary

____

Add the missing commas to these sentences.

10–11 Grandad who was feeling grumpy anyway got really cross when the puppy chewed his new slippers.

12–13 Take a few moments to listen to different sounds – perhaps the sound of the wind howling sirens screaming leaves rustling or buzzing planes.

14 To be able to understand your own beliefs and values you need to learn about the beliefs and values of others.

Add two suffixes to each of these to make new words.

15–16 friend __________ __________

17–18 shame __________ __________

19–20 happy __________ __________

21–22 pain __________ __________

23–24 great __________ __________

Write three sentences, one with a colon, one with a semicolon and one with a colon introducing a list using three semicolons.

25 __________

26 __________

27–30 __________

Total

TEST 15: **Vocabulary**

Test time: 0 5 10 minutes

Write each of these words in a sentence.

withhold

1 ____________________

access

2 ____________________

opportunity

3 ____________________

persistence

4 ____________________

mischievous

5 ____________________

Write the masculine gender of each of these words.

6 wife ____________

7 princess ____________

8 niece ____________

9 lady ____________

10 lioness ____________

11 vixen ____________

Circle the words that have come into the English language since 1900.

12–15

chimney television box

pottery DVD player glass astronaut

bicycle website mantelpiece

Write these *abbreviations* in full.

16 CD ______________________

17 kg ______________________

18 USA ______________________

19 SE ______________________

20 MP ______________________

Fill the gaps with two words. The four words in each set need to be in alphabetical order.

21–22 outback ____________ ____________ outsider

23–24 thread ____________ ____________ thrush

25–26 disease ____________ ____________ distress

Write a *metaphor* for each of these subjects.

27 wind

____

28 snow

____

29 leaves

____

30 bedroom

____

Total

TEST 16: **Mixed**

Test time: 0 5 10 minutes

List the four different types of noun. Write an example of each.

1–2 ______________ noun Example: ______________

3–4 ______________ noun Example: ______________

5–6 ______________ noun Example: ______________

7–8 ______________ noun Example: ______________

Write these sentences as *direct speech*.

9 Mum called to Ben that it was time to put the chips in the oven.

____

10 The vet told me there was nothing to worry about.

____

11 Mrs Owen announced it was time for lunch.

____

12 Ryan asked Rupesh if he would like to stay the night at his house.

____

____

Write five sentences. In each sentence use the listed word or phrase correctly.

13 man eating shark ______________________________

14 hot-water bottle ______________________________

15 recover ______________________________

16 small-business manager ______________________________

17 heavy metal detector ______________________________

Write a *simile* using the following subjects.

18 water

____

19 swan

____

20 drum

____

21 spider

____

22 monkey

____

Write the *root word* of each of these words.

23 submarine ____________

24 exclaim ____________

25 postage ____________

26 digestible ____________

27 reliable ____________

28 international ____________

29 hygienic ____________

30 offensive ____________

Time for a break! Go to Puzzle Page 45

Total

Test 17: Grammar

Test time: 0 5 10 minutes

Add a different verb and *adverb* to each sentence.

1–2 Fiona ______________ ______________ to the other side of the playground.

3–4 The postman ______________ ______________ in the rain.

5–6 The abandoned dog ______________ ______________ for his home.

7–8 The bird ______________ ______________ on her eggs waiting for them to hatch.

9–10 Mrs Seal's class ______________ ______________ as they waited for lunch.

Complete these sentences. Use a *conjunction* from the box in each one. You may use each word only once.

because	but	if	when	and

11 Molly loved her party dress ______________________________

____

12 Reuben had saved his pocket money for weeks ______________________

____

13 Bill and Jake planned to meet in town ______________________________

____

14 The snake watched the mouse ______________________________

____

15 The sheep escaped from their field ______________________________

____

Write an *adjectival phrase* about each of these nouns.

16 a banana

____

17 the children

____

18 a spider

____

19 the wind

____

20 a computer game

____

Write two examples of each of the following.

21–22 abstract noun ______________ ______________

23–24 preposition ______________ ______________

25–26 verb ______________ ______________

27–28 pronoun ______________ ______________

29–30 superlative adjective ______________ ______________

Total

Test time: 0 5 10 minutes

Read this extract carefully.

Hurricane Summer *by Robert Swindells*

Funny things, friendships. They tend to come and go, but most people have a special friend who stands out among all the others. I'm lucky – I've got two. One of them's been dead a long time now, but it doesn't matter – he'll always be my friend. As for the other ... well, as I said, friendships are funny. Best thing I can do is tell you about them.

The Second World War was on and I was ten. I was an only child. My dad had been killed the previous autumn serving with the Navy. Mum said I must always remember that my dad had been a hero, and I knew he had, that was the trouble.

You see, I wasn't a hero. Far from it.

There was this lad at school. Clive Simcox. He was the same age as me – we were in the same class – but Clive was taller and heavier, and for some reason that summer he started picking on me. I didn't like fighting so I was forever trying to please him. I let him win at marbles and lent him my wicket keeper's gloves. I even gave him my best stamp – a Guadeloupe triangular – but it was no use. He'd still ambush me on the way home from school and bash me up. He used to wait for me in the mornings too, and trip me as I ran past. I'd arrive at school with grazed knees and dirt on my blazer and red eyes from crying, and everybody would know Clive had had another go at me.

He used to make remarks about my Dad, which was even worse. Before the war Dad had been an electrician, so they made him an electrician in the Navy. I don't know what his work was exactly, but it had to do with electrical circuits and that sort of thing. Anyway, Clive had latched on to this and sometimes he'd say, "He **was nothing special**, you know, your dad. He wasn't a gunner or a torpedo man. He didn't kill any Germans. He was just an electrician, mending fuses and changing lightbulbs while other fellows did the fighting." This would be in the playground or on the street and he'd say it at the top of his voice so everyone could hear, and all the time he'd be pushing me – shoving me in the chest so that I had to keep stepping backwards. He was goading me of course – trying to make me fight, but I was too scared. Red-faced with shame, I'd retreat till he got bored and went off to bother somebody else.

I **despised** myself. I'd think, what sort of kid doesn't stick up for his dead father? Defend his honour? If I was half the hero Dad was, I'd stand up to Simcox and punch him on the nose, even if he bashed me up after ... When it came to it – when he was actually there in front of me with his red face and mocking eyes – I'd either try to run or let him hit me to get it over. I was ashamed of myself but I couldn't help it.

Funniest thing was, Simcox senior wasn't even in the forces. He worked in a button factory, but I daren't bring that up when Clive was tormenting me. Shows how scared I was, and believe me it's no joke being a coward when the world seems **full of heroes**.

Answer these questions about the extract.

1 In which war had the boy's father died? ______________________

2 List the three ways the boy tried to please Clive Simcox.

____

____

3 How did everyone know when Clive had bullied the boy?

____

4 Why did Clive Simcox believe the boy's father **'was nothing special'**?

____

5 In your own words describe why the boy **'despised'** himself.

____

6 What did Clive Simcox's dad do during the war?

____

7 How do you think Clive Simcox felt while bullying the boy?

____

____

8 Why do you think Clive Simcox was a bully?

____

____

9 When you see someone being bullied how do you feel?

____

____

10 Why did the world seem **'full of heroes'**?

____

____

Total

Test 19: Mixed

Test time: 0 5 10 minutes

Write the meaning of each of these proverbs.

1 Two heads are better than one.

2 Practice makes perfect.

3 You scratch my back and I'll scratch yours.

4 Let sleeping dogs lie.

Rewrite these sentences with the missing punctuation.

5–11 Can I open my present now asked Gina I have waited a very long time

12–16 Lets go ice-skating suggested Jenny

Write two *onomatopoeic* words that can describe each of these.

17–18 an avalanche ____________ ____________

19–20 a snake ____________ ____________

21–22 a firework ____________ ____________

What parts of speech are each of these words?

23 it ____________

24 but ____________

25 grumpily ____________

26 hate ____________

27 remove ____________

Write an example of each of the following.

28 a question

____

29 a statement

____

30 a command

____

Total

TEST 20: **Sentences**

Test time: 0 5 10 minutes

Add 'was' or 'were' to each sentence to make it correct.

1 The Jacob family __________ relieved to reach their holiday home.

2 The dog barked excitedly every time the ball __________ thrown to him.

3 Mrs Trevis's children __________ very well-behaved during the concert.

4 Half the audience cheered when the villain __________ caught.

5 Hannah __________ too excited to sleep.

Complete each sentence with a *phrase* or *clause*.

6 The horses ____

____ waited for their morning feed.

7 Ben rode his bike ____

____ to Tuhil's house.

8 Rebecca ____

____ waited for her brother.

Write two sentences that include a *relative clause*.

9 ____

10 ____

Rewrite these sentences correctly.

11–15 quieten down bellowed the headteacher

____

16–18 darren raced towards the ball not wanting to be beaten by anyone

____

____

19–23 are we going to win called Helen

____

____

Write three sentences using the passive voice. Remember, a sentence is written in the passive voice when the subject of the sentence has an action done to it by someone or something else.

24 ____

25 ____

26 ____

Circle the letters in these sentences that need capitals.

27 dave's cats, batman and robin, tore up his harry potter poster.

28 the train was late, eventually arriving in manchester after manchester united had won their match!

Time for a break! Go to Puzzle Page 46

Total

Puzzle 1

In each of these groups of letters there are two words muddled together but with the letters placed in the correct order.

Can you sort the muddled words?

All capital letters are missing. Use the clues to help.

1 asfroiutcha
(a country) ____________ ____________

2 sdtepoarrtmenet
(a type of shop) ____________ ____________

3 dsotwrneientg
(a place in London) ____________ ____________

4 crpeanciylon
(can be used to mark paper) ____________ ____________

5 strhoopplIienyg
(used in a supermarket) ____________ ____________

6 wprirlnlicame
(a famous person) ____________ ____________

7 csoswitmumimnge
(needed when doing the crawl or breaststroke) ____________ ____________

8 bpeltueer
(a television programme) ____________ ____________

Write some muddled words and clues of your own.

Try them out on someone.

A ____

____

B ____

____

Puzzle 2

Find four soft c and four soft g words in this wordsearch.

b	k	r	e	c	e	i	v	e	v
n	d	g	n	s	t	m	d	f	e
e	g	a	o	l	f	a	c	n	g
c	x	k	c	a	k	g	o	g	e
e	r	e	l	i	g	i	o	n	t
s	a	d	b	t	s	n	b	s	a
s	f	d	n	i	d	a	d	n	b
a	n	s	c	b	s	t	n	t	l
r	c	e	t	o	z	i	m	b	e
y	d	o	g	n	d	o	c	g	a
i	n	n	o	c	e	n	t	o	k

Write the words you have found.

soft c words

____

____

____

____

soft g words

____

____

____

____

Puzzle 3

How many words can you find from the same word family?

spark	happy	phone
spark**ler**		
spark**ling**		
spark**le**		

question	detect	graph

Puzzle 4

As time passes more and more words are being invented.

For example the word 'cheeseburger' was invented to describe a hamburger that had cheese added to it.

Invent your own words for:

a hovering skateboard ______________________

a jam and ham sandwich ______________________

someone who always walks backwards ______________________

an animal that speaks ______________________

someone who can fly ______________________

a pot plant that asks for water when it needs it ______________________

Invent three more words with your own definitions.

____

____

____

Puzzle 5

Complete the crossword.

Each of the answers begins with a number prefix.
The clues will help you!

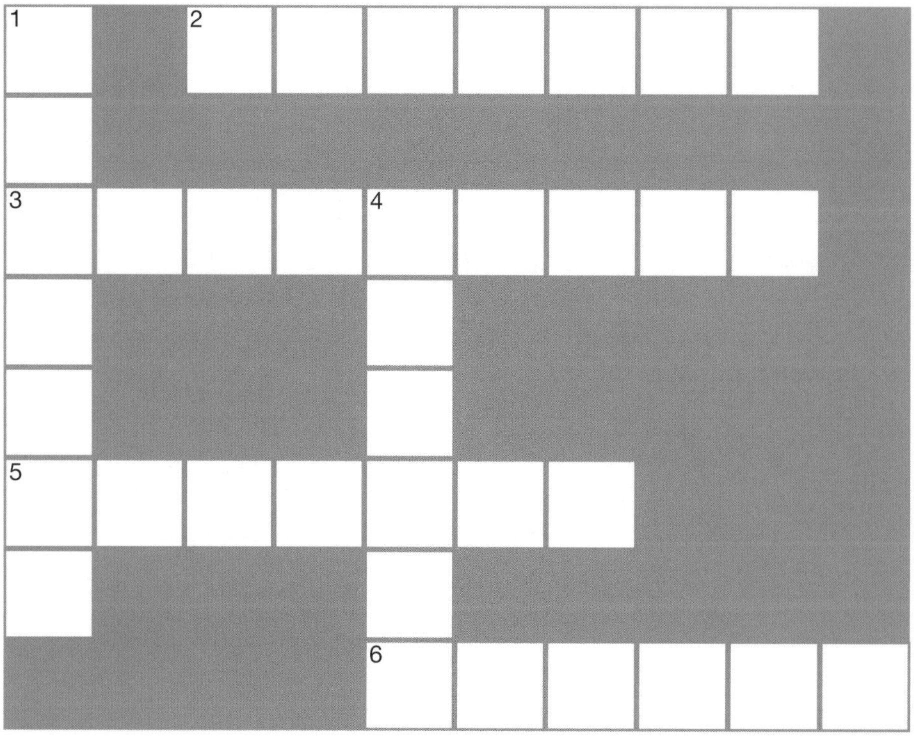

Across

2 A two-wheeled vehicle.

3 A race in three parts.

5 An underwater animal with eight tentacles.

6 Ten years.

Down

1 A shape with eight sides.

4 A stand often used with a camera.

Key words

Some special words are used in this book. You will find them picked out in *italics*. These words are explained here.

abbreviation	a word that has been shortened
abstract noun	a noun referring to a concept or idea, e.g. love, beauty
adjectival phrase	a group of words describing a noun
adjective	a word that describes somebody or something
adverb	a word that gives extra meaning to a verb
adverbial phrase	a word or phrase that makes the meaning of a verb, adjective or another adverb more specific, e.g. The Cheshire cat vanished *quite slowly*, beginning with the end of its tail
antonym	a word with a meaning opposite to another word, e.g. hot/cold
clause	a section of a sentence with a verb
collective noun	a noun referring to a group or collection of things, e.g. a swarm of bees
comparative	describes the amount of something (adverb or adjective), e.g. more, bigger
conjunction	a word used to link sentences, phrases or words, e.g. and, but
contraction	two words shortened into one with an apostrophe placed where the letter/s have been dropped, e.g. do not/don't
diminutive	a word implying smallness, e.g. duckling
fronted adverbial	an adverbial that has been moved before the verb, e.g. *The day after tomorrow*, I'm going on holiday
homophone	a word that has the same sound as another but a different meaning or spelling, e.g. right/write
idiom	a phrase that is not meant literally
infinitive	the basic form of the verb, e.g. to scream
indirect speech	what has been said without using the exact words or inverted commas
metaphor	a figurative expression in which something is described in terms usually associated with something else, e.g. the sky is a sapphire sea
mnemonic	a way of aiding the memory, e.g. a rhyme or silly story
modal verb	verbs that change the meaning of other verbs, e.g. can, will
onomatopoeic	a word that echoes a sound, associated with its meaning, e.g. hiss
parenthesis	this is a word or phrase that is separated off from the main sentence by brackets, commas or dashes usually because it contains additional information not essential to its understanding
phrase	a group of words that do not contain both a subject and a verb
preposition	a word that links nouns and pronouns to other parts of a sentence, e.g. he sat *behind* the door
pronoun	a word that can be used instead of a noun
relative clause	a special type of subordinate clause that makes the meaning of a noun more specific, e.g. The prize *that I won* was a book
root word	a word to which a prefix or suffix can be added to make another word, e.g. quick – *quick*ly
simile	an expression to describe what something is like, e.g. as cold as ice
superlative	describes the limit of a quality (adjective or adverb), e.g. most, least, shortest
synonym	a word with a very similar meaning to another word, e.g. quick/fast

Progress Grid

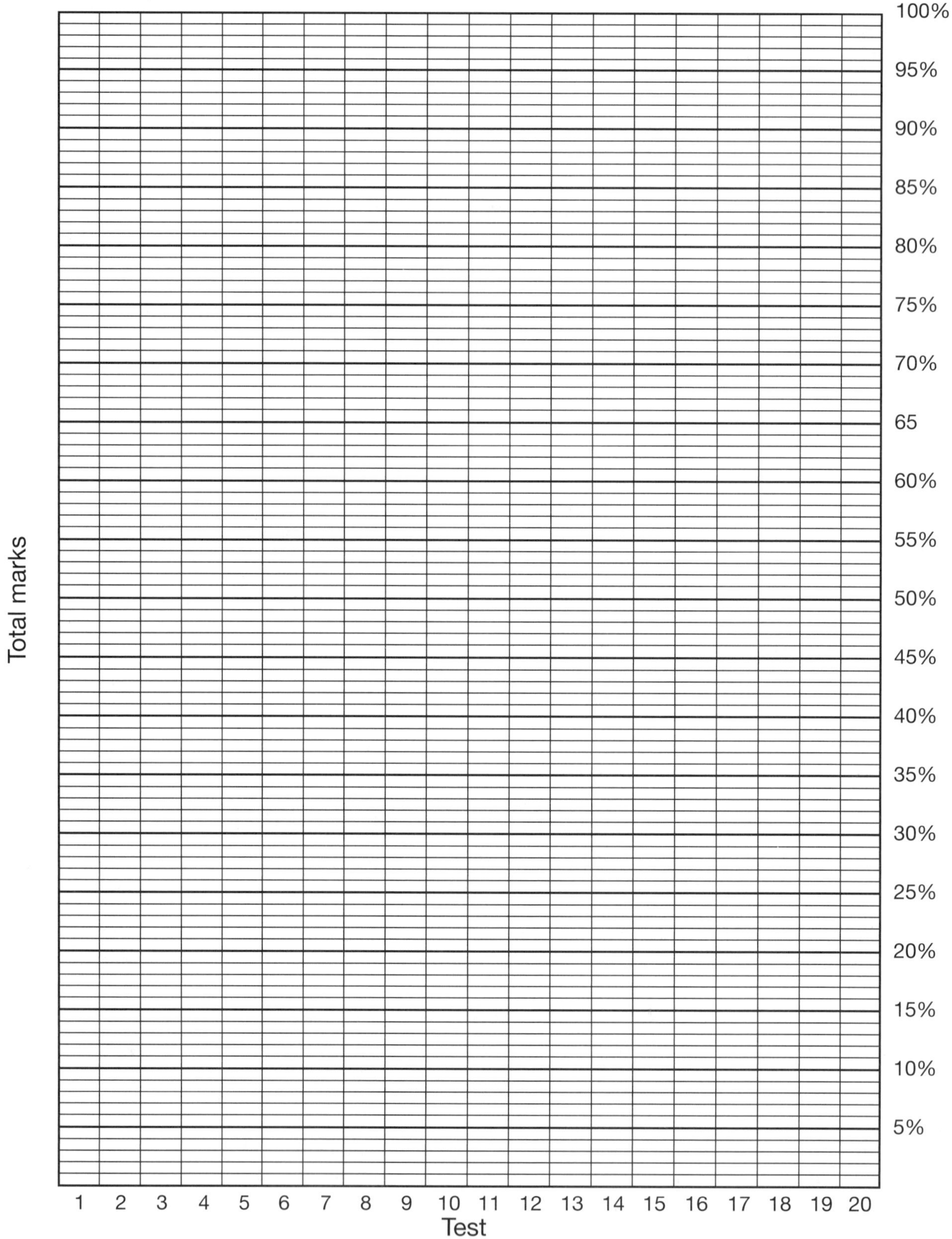